Purchasing Information:
Paperback available from www.AdHocFiction.com
E-book available from all usual outlets.

Printed in the United Kingdom.
First Printing 2020.

ISBN paperback 978-1-912095-79-7
ISBN e-Book 978-1-912095-78-0

# GOING SHORT

## An Invitation to Flash Fiction

by Nancy Stohlman

*to all my teachers*
*and all my students*
*may we always be both*

# Advanced Praise

"In *Going Short*, Nancy Stohlman captures the true spirit of flash fiction, those brief narratives imbued with all the urgency of life itself. An extremely practiced flash fiction writer, Stohlman is also a veteran teacher. She knows the territory and takes us on a trip from getting started to the finishing line, and everything in between. It's hard to think of a more thoughtful, adept, and enthusiastic guide."
~David Galef, author of *Brevity: A Flash Fiction Handbook*

"Nancy Stohlman has written the definitive, and appropriately concise, book on the flash fiction form. You'll learn what flash fiction is and isn't, tips on writing it, tips on honing, sculpting, and polishing it (I especially like her idea of "swapping" sentences and paragraphs in revision and "strategic cutting"), along with thoughtful discussions on the flash novel and tips for pulling together a flash collection. As a widely-published master of the form herself, Stohlman brings years of teaching experience and her own engaging voice and wit to this useful, encouraging, and entertaining guide. A must-have for flash writers of all levels."
~Kathy Fish, author of *Wild Life: Collected Works 2003-2018*

"*Going Short* embraces the urgency and compression of flash in presenting specific, fresh suggestions for creating, drafting, revising, editing, and publishing both individual pieces and full collections. It's a book that knows and teaches by doing. It is inspiring and insightful, a masterful craft book written by a master of the craft."

~Randall Brown, author of *This Is How He Learned to Love*

# Foreword

"This book is an invitation to flash dance with Nancy Stohlman, an accomplished partner who will show you the steps you can take, the fluid moves you can make on the flash fiction studio floor.

It is all about practice.

She will spin you around and show you things you didn't know you could do, and lead you to a kind of prose performance you didn't think possible.

It's all about paying close attention and getting it down with the necessary urgency.

It's not easy at first, it's a tricky art form, but Nancy shares her sharp insight and offers short cuts to get you more quickly to your own satisfaction and your reader's delight.

And at the studio door when it's time to leave, she hands you a scroll of a hundred good ideas and wishes you happy travels. Just follow the map."

~*James Thomas*, Co-editor of the Norton *Flash Fiction* books

# Contents

# INTRODUCTION

## Going Short

Flash fiction arrived in my life as I was writing my third novel, agonizing over it like a relationship you really *really* want to work out, dammit. And, after so many years of writing more—talk *more* about this, give *more* description here, *more* backstory here, explain this *more*—it was such a relief to write less. Because I never really wanted to say all that other stuff anyway.

Flash fiction is changing the way we tell stories. Carving away the excess, eliminating all but the most essential, flash fiction is putting the story through a literary dehydrator, leaving the meat without the fat. Readers are discovering something delightful and poignant in these little spaces. Writers are cultivating a new set of skills and writing a different kind of story. And the stories, far from lazy or trivial, have their finger on a new and necessary urgency.

Before the term "flash fiction" (thanks to James Thomas and Robert Shapard), stories under 1,000 words were often marooned in a wasteland—not long enough to be taken seriously or compete with their hefty siblings. But in the last 25 years, flash fiction has become not only a legitimate genre but a movement. Making use of tools like erasure, ambiguity and implication, it has reinvented *how* we tell a story. And it only looks easy.

Every now and then someone will read one of my stories and tell me with great enthusiasm: you could turn this into a whole novel! I know it's meant to be a compliment. But sometimes the more you know about something, the less you like it. George Saunders said in an interview once that many of his stories started out as novels until he "came to his senses." And certain stories should become novels, should become long-term relationships with all their nuances.

But flash fiction saved me from writing all those novels. Sometimes it's just the single snippet of conversation that haunts you—that brief and dazzling moment when your life intersects with the story before it continues on without you.

# ARE YOU FLASH-CURIOUS?

## What's Flash Fiction?

Flash fictions are stories under 1,000 words. And flash fiction is always telling a story, even if much of that story is implied.

While flash fiction is the most widely used term, and 1,000 words the most widely used word limit, there are other names: sudden fiction, nanofiction, short-shorts. Recently microfiction has become a subgenre for stories under 300-ish words, and there are journals and books that specialize in stories that are 100 words, 50 words, even just one sentence.

# Does It Have to Be Fiction?

Not necessarily.

Whether something's written as fact or fiction comes down to the author. If you're a journalist, or a historian, or you're writing a memoir or a travel article, facts are important. But if you just want to tell stories, and some of those stories are rooted in real world events but that's not the point, then maybe it wants to be fiction.

I'll be using the terms "flash" and "flash fiction" interchangeably for stories (under 1,000 words) that are born in reality...and in the imagination...and everything in between.

# Why Should I Write Flash Fiction?

Writing flash fiction will make you a better writer. Period.

Whether you're seasoned in other genres or new to writing altogether, there's so much to be learned from the skills of flash fiction: brevity, urgency, compression, and discernment, as well as embracing constraints and the freedom that comes from creative risk taking. Flash fiction will change you. It will make you a very different writer. You'll cultivate a sharper instinct to what's truly necessary in your work.

# Isn't That a Prose Poem? Don't You Mean Vignette?

No, no no no no.

Just because a piece of writing is under 1,000 words doesn't mean it's flash fiction.

What's the difference?

Urgency.

Flash fiction is *always* telling a story.

# PART ONE

# WRITING FLASH FICTION

# The Blank Page

So you want to write flash fiction?

Let go of being good at it. It takes a while to get used to a new form, and it can feel frustrating to "start over" as a beginner. Consider it an opportunity.

Let go of your tricks and your clever exposition techniques.

Let go of your need to explain. Discover what you *don't* need to say.

Let go of description—one perfect detail will do the trick.

Let silences be potent…don't rush to fill them.

Let go of extra words: create meaningful gaps.

Let go of the urge to linger.

So what's left?

What's left is a tightly crafted nugget of concentrated gold.

What's left is flash fiction.

# Urgency

Writers arrive at flash fiction with different strengths and weaknesses. Prose writers, including novelists, memoirists, and short story writers, are usually comfortable with narrative but can struggle with the word constraint. Poets are usually good working in small spaces, but they can struggle with narrative, creating vignettes or prose poems that may or may not be telling a story.

A good story has urgency. Something has to happen.

The flash fiction story bends with tension like a fish caught at the end of a pole. There's movement, a sense of something unfolding—or having just unfolded. Consider: a woman at a café watching the fall leaves shimmer in the sun could be a prose poem or a vignette or even a character study. But a woman at a café watching the fall leaves shimmer in the sun—as a man in overalls is sawing through the trunk—is a story.

Can't poetry tell a story? Of course. Can't flash fiction be poetic? Absolutely. But the answer lies in the driving force of a piece: prose poetry and vignettes are *driven* by imagery and emotion whereas flash fiction is driven by narrative. Neither prose poems nor vignettes are at the mercy of plot, while flash fiction has an almost desperate need to *tell a story before it's too late.*

# The Zoom Lens

One of my favorite approaches to writing a flash fiction story is what I call the zoom lens—taking an ultra close-up shot of what's potentially a much bigger story. It's like narrowing the focus from a wide-angle landscape to a single flower. In flash fiction, the single flower can be the whole world.

To begin, make a list of stories or potential stories you intend to write/rewrite. Now for each of these stories identify the actual timeline—how much chronological time does this story cover from beginning to end? A week? Three weeks? A year? An hour? Several months? One day? Ten years?

Once you've decided, ask yourself: what's the most important *5 minutes*?

Now write that and only that.

When you zoom, the whole story happens in one frame. There's no room for backstory or extraneous description. Resist the urge to explain anything, no flashbacks or other tricks of exposition—just "drop" us into that little slice of story.

Five minutes later, leave.

# Implicating the Reader

There are only two "rules" to flash fiction: it should be 1,000 words or less, and it should tell a story. But how can you tell an entire story in such a small space—sometimes as few as 50 words?

We do it through very purposeful *implication*. As writers, we can imply all sorts of things—from action to description to backstory. For instance—if I tell you I just flushed the toilet, I'm implying and you'll assume I just used the bathroom. If tell you I sat on the porch, you'll assume I had to open the door and walk outside. If I tell you I got on an airplane, then you'll assume I had to arrive at the airport, check my luggage, etc. A writer doesn't have to describe the security check or the turning of the front door handle as long as they are *obvious* assumptions.

Now if I was flushing a gun down the toilet or getting on a private jet, I would need to explain.

Entire settings can be implied. One writer sets his stories in places like airports or hotels so he *doesn't* have to describe the setting. "Airport" and "hotel" are familiar and already bring up a host of implied descriptions. But if the airport is filled with goats or the hotel concierge has a glass eye—you better describe that.

# Flash Dialogue

Dialogue is an important part of all good writing. But in flash fiction, where you have limited space for description or backstory, it can become the entire story. So you really have to get it right.

Dialogue tends to either be a strength or a weakness for most writers. In my case it used to be a weakness—I wrote dialogue that sounded like caricature for years. It wasn't until I started purposefully eavesdropping that I finally started to get it: how you *think* people talk vs how they actually talk.

Most of us think we already know how people talk until we start listening. How people put their sentences together, for instance, is as unique as their fingerprints. We can easily tell the difference between someone from Louisiana and someone from London, but only because it's exaggerated. Once you start paying attention, even two people from the same city will sound different.

The best way to improve your dialogue is to carry around a notebook and start transcribing (public!) conversations: on the bus, on the train, in the hallways. The goal is to get it *word for word,* which usually means writing fast. And don't worry if you don't get the entire conversation from beginning to end—you probably won't.

Even if you're a master of dialogue, even if you've done similar exercises, I encourage you to get out there and do it again. Not only is it good practice in creative play, but you may find that you're given the rare and perfect gift of a complete flash fiction piece just by paying attention.

# Is My Story Too Long? Embracing Constraints

My story is just over 1,000 words—too long for flash?

The answer is technically yes (though I've occasionally seen flash defined as 1,200 or even 1,500 words), but I've found that a story coming in at 999 words is usually written by someone who's still trying to "make it fit."

Writers new to flash often find the constraint arbitrary and infuriating: *why such a stickler on the word count? So what if it's a few words over?* But I believe the magic of flash fiction happens *because* of the constraint. Interesting things bulge against boundaries. From sonnets to prompts—even deadlines—many writers find they produce their best work when pushing against a constraint: you can only paint with the color green, you must finish a film in 48 hours, you have to write a story without using the letter E. Beethoven wrote his most important symphony when he was deaf.

Embracing the constraint is the true gift of flash fiction.

So, if your first attempts are ending up at 999 words, don't worry. The more comfortable you get, the more your stories will naturally shrink. Here's how you'll know you've crossed over: you'll never need to look at the word count again.

# The Bedtime Story

Once upon a time, there was a story that had to be told quickly...

When we tell (or listen to) a bedtime story, there's an assumption that we'll finish in one sitting. Rather than zooming into one 5-minute slice of the plot, The Bedtime Story takes a different narrative approach and tells the entire story from beginning to end without leaving anything out...but it moves quickly.

Some of the best examples are fairy tales. The fairy tale as a genre might even be rightly considered a precursor to flash fiction because fairy tales are often told in 1,000 words or less and always tell a complete story with a beginning, middle, and end. In order to accomplish this feat, the story focuses on just one plotline and doesn't take tangents, a swift but even jaunt from A to B, pointing out the important, need-to-know sights but not lingering to take pictures.

And it works. At the end of a fairy tale we aren't left asking: what is Red Riding Hood's relationship with her mother like? Where is her father? What kind of childhood did Goldilocks have? How did Hansel and Gretel adjust after their kidnapping? We don't ask these questions because they're not important to the story. It *is* important to know the length and color of Rapunzel's hair, but we don't need to know what Red Riding Hood looks like at all.

The reader is forgiving of the things left out in favor of the urgency and swiftness required. And as a bonus, that accelerated rhythm helps contribute to the tension, the feeling that we are indeed going somewhere.

The End.

# Bribing the Muse: On Your Mark, Get Set...

A great way to create a sense of urgency in a flash fiction story is by using another constraint: time.

For almost a decade now, all my college classes have begun with a 10-minute timed writing. Timed writing is nothing new. We know that it helps us transition us into the writing space, like stretching before a workout. We know that it forces us to stay present and dig deeper—writing past where we might have naturally given up. And we know that keeping the pen moving quickly, without crossing things out or rereading, is a great way to evade the internal critic and uncover fresh ideas.

But I discovered something else through years of this practice: 10 minutes of writing without stopping is also the *perfect* amount of time to draft a flash fiction story idea from start to finish.

It makes sense: if flash fiction is defined by a word constraint, why not create under a time constraint? Having that clock ticking while you furiously try to reach the end of an idea gives the piece a natural sense of urgency. And writing from the beginning to the end in one sitting also creates a sense of continuity—we see the end coming as we embark on the journey.

You can use timed writing in many ways. For instance, you can:

- Set the timer while writing to a prompt.
- Set the timer when you're feeling stuck and don't know what to write about.
- Set the timer and rewrite a "flat" story from scratch while the clock chases you to the finish line (my favorite).

As a daily practice it's even better. Besides, you can do anything for 10 minutes, right?

# Bribing the Muse: Flash Flood

Bad writing creeps into flash fiction as it creeps into all genres. It happens to the beginner and the professional equally. In fact, if you haven't produced any bad writing lately, then you probably haven't been writing enough.

If you write a lot, much will be bad, but there will also be the seeds of really good work. Anne Lamott says in *Bird by Bird,* "There may be something in the very last line of the very last paragraph on page six that you just love, that is so beautiful or wild that you now know what you're supposed to be writing about, more or less, or in what direction you might go—but there was no way to get to this without first getting through the first five and a half pages."

So write a lot, and write badly.

I write in notebooks, longhand, every day, and 90 percent of what I write in there is bad. I fill a notebook with bad writing every month or two. To some that might seem like a complete waste of time. But for me it's about staying limber: the trick is to be in shape, to be warmed up and loose so when the good stuff does arrive you're ready.

# Found Forms: Literary Squatters

One of my favorite approaches to writing flash fiction is to use a ready-made container—a constraint we'll call a "found form."

Hermit crabs, foxes, turtles, owls and other animal squatters "borrow" the homes of existing animals rather than build their own. When using found forms you borrow a pre-built structure in the same way.

A found form is any "non-literary" form that contains text: junk mail, newsletters, notes from school, grocery lists, your child's homework, recipes, how-to manuals. It could include contracts, leases, court documents, instructions, classifieds, online sources such as emails and websites, obituaries, legal paperwork, newspaper articles, brochures, company memos, letters to the editor, product information, disclaimers and more. If you walk outside a middle school after the final bell you are sure to find plenty of "found text" on the ground—notes, tests, love letters.

Borrowing these forms can be an interesting and effective way to tell a story in a restricted space. For instance, writing a story in the form of "divorce proceedings" can be far more insightful to a reader than trying to relay an entire relationship chronologically.

So keep your eyes open. You never know what great ideas for writing you can get from seemingly non-literary sources.

# Flash Myth #1: Smaller Is Easier

Let's debunk Myth #1.

Housed in the Chicago Institute of Art are the Thorne Miniature Rooms, tiny replicas of actual historic rooms painstakingly crafted on a scale of one inch: one foot. You press your face up to each of the 68 windows and gaze at the fully formed world inside— complete with exotic woods, fabrics, chandeliers and intricate, hand-woven rugs. The attention to detail in each room would be impressive even at life size, but the true fascination is the fact that they are just so damn tiny!

One of the reasons people love flash fiction is because, like the Thorne Rooms, there is something awe-inspiring about entering a perfectly formed tiny world. When done correctly, tiny is part of the art: the *Mona Lisa* on a grain of rice, a sculpture of Charlie Chaplin balanced on an eyelash. And it often requires *more* skill from the writer, not the other way around. Creating something tiny takes a different level of expertise and precision.

Sometimes when people discover flash fiction they assume: oh, it's cute, it's small, it's easy. But to fully appreciate flash we must assume mastery: the story is small because the author has *decided to tell it this way.*

# Flash Myth #2: Readers Have Short Attention Spans

This is probably the most common flash myth. But readers aren't enamored with flash fiction because they have short attentions spans—that's like saying the sculptor of the bonsai tree didn't have the attention for a full-grown tree, or that people who eat sliders don't have the attention for a quarter-pound hamburger. Maybe, just maybe, they *like* sliders and bonsai trees?

In the same way, readers love flash fiction because it's complex and breathtaking and accomplishes *so much* in such a tiny space.

In fact, flash fiction requires a more sophisticated reader. The story demands the reader to "pay close attention"—every sentence, every word takes on a new significance, if only for the limited number of them. The reader must jump the gaps, fill in the blanks, follow the breadcrumbs, and inhabit the purposeful spaces left by the writer. Which means that flash fiction is cultivating a new symbiosis between writer and readers, on and off the page.

As readers, we've gotten used to sitting in the audience and being entertained. But it's nearly impossible to passively consume flash fiction. Leaving things unsaid and undigested requires effort and interpretation; the reader steps out of the role of voyeur and becomes an active participant in the story. It's this act of interpretation that keeps art vital—no longer just watching from a darkened audience, flash fiction invites the reader up on the stage, hands them a tambourine, and tells them to keep up.

# Flash Myth #3: Bigger Is Better

"Important" literary works are big. Therefore, some people still dismiss flash fiction as trivial. How could anything important be accomplished in such a small space? Flash fiction is good for barroom bets, not for serious literature.

The implication here is the *more* we have of something, the better it is. *War and Peace* is "important": it's long, it's hard, it's complex, it's 1,200 pages. But *Old Man and the Sea* is only 120 pages and won the Nobel Prize for Literature. Should we assume that Tolstoy worked 10x harder than Hemingway or that his work is 10x more important?

The truth is they can't really be compared.

Flash fiction should be judged on its own terms. It's meant to be digested in one sitting—it encourages speed, not languishing. Longer literature is meant to be enjoyed over time. But flash fiction doesn't look for sweeping vistas. Flash fiction is not the epic saga. Flash fiction is that guy on the beach with the metal detector. We don't need to know his history, we don't need to know what he looks like. Just tell us what he finds.

# I Was a Flash Fraud

I'll be honest: I had a hard time going short. After more than 10 years writing novels, my first "flash" stories were cannibalized from various longer projects, fixed with new titles, and called flash. And this sort of worked, for a minute, but it felt like cheating (and it was). I hadn't really *written* flash at all.

I think most writers spend some transitional time as flash frauds. Eventually you run out of excerpts or longer stories to butcher or prose poems to pass off and are forced to do what you should be doing from the beginning—conceiving stories in flash. I knew when I finally wrote a real flash piece: it felt different. And once I started "seeing in flash," the stories were all around me like 3D images emerging from an optical illusion—finally presenting themselves.

# High-Wire Flips and Narrative Contortions

Flash fiction has created a new sort of genre freedom with only one rule: tell us a story in 1,000 words. I don't care how you do it. Just make it work.

As a result, flash fiction stories are attempting contortions that wouldn't work elsewhere, a circus of tightrope walkers and jugglers and trapeze artists, plunging against their boundaries. Writers are taking risks and experimenting with narrative precisely because what might become gimmicky in a longer piece will work for flash *because it is short.*

Writer Kathy Fish explains: "With so few words at its disposal, flash fiction lends itself beautifully to innovation and experimentation. All those extra words we must do without force flash writers to find other ways to create a fully realized story, complete with emotion, movement, and resonance."

So many of the joys of both writing and reading flash fiction are the literary acrobatics that happen when plots are forced to bend in such small spaces. Flash stories can be circular, change tenses or points of view, told as monologues or in a found form, told backwards or completely in dialogue. A flash story might be one long circular breathless sentence. We are telling stories that *could not be told in any other form.*

As a writer, that's incredibly exciting.

# Bribing the Muse: The All-Night Diner of Inspiration

According to *The Surrealist Manifesto,* Saint-Pol-Roux is said to have posted a sign on the door before he went to sleep every night that read: 'THE POET IS WORKING.'

Over the years I've probably gotten half my ideas from dreaming. Usually it's just a wisp or a random image or a line of dialogue, but sometimes the whole story rises out of the dream ether in one piece, fully formed, usually in that transition time between asleep and awake when the muse is still whispering in my ear and I haven't sabotaged her yet.

In dreams the ego is gone; it's just you and your imagination, a highly creative conversation with your subconscious, an all-night diner of free inspiration. And the ideas are completely original, completely yours.

Even if you think you don't dream, you do. But dream material only works if you learn to speak its language and approach it on its own territory. I suggest keeping a notebook next to your bed and write down *anything* (even the smallest thing) you remember as soon as you wake. If you must, write:

"I remember nothing." But write something. The act of writing is a message to your subconscious: I need more details.

Try it. You'll be amazed how the subconscious will oblige. The key is to be vigilant, to catch these little gifts and write them down before they're gone, and don't ask yourself "is this crazy?" because it probably is. And that's good.

# Bribing the Muse: Using Prompts

Writers have been using prompts for many years. Consider: a classic form such as the sonnet—with its very specific rhyme pattern and number of lines—is essentially a prompt.

You may already know about the Oulipo Movement, which started in 1960's Paris and began what we now call the French New Wave. Oulipo was a group of artists and mathematicians who purposefully worked within (random) constraints to uncover new kinds of art. George Perec, for instance, wrote a brilliant book, *La Disparition (The Void)*, without using the letter "e," and one of Oulipo's more famous prompts was N + 7, which replaces all the nouns in a piece of writing with the word seven entries later in the dictionary.

I like to think of these founders of *Ouvroir de Litterature Potentielle* (OULIPO), or Workshop of Potential Literature, as forerunners of the flash fiction movement because they believed in the "profound potential of a poem produced within a framework or formula and that, if done in a playful posture, the outcomes could be endless."

Playful potential is the beauty of prompts—they take us into new territory. And, not coincidentally, it's also the beauty of flash fiction: to create new outcomes inspired by and written within seemingly random constraints.

I've included 100 FlashNano prompts at the end of this book.

# Microfiction: Literary Peep Shows

And what about microfiction? How is that different?

Microfiction is to flash fiction what flash fiction is to the short story. Again, no hard and fast definitions here (and we like it that way), but if flash is 1,000 words or less, then microfiction is roughly 300 words or less. And eventually you may find that even 300 words seems so long!

If the flash story is 5 minutes, the micro is 1 minute. It's a literary peep show, a momentary glimpse—the curtain lifts and a fully-formed world is framed inside the panes of glass. Your brain must very quickly tell a story about what it sees: why is that woman covered in blood? Why is that child buying so much spinach? What is that man going to do with that flyswatter? What prompted a "No Kissing Zone" sign at the Costa Rica bus station?

Writing microfiction requires you to come even closer to the story. That said, you can still use the same narrative approaches but in miniature. Observe:

*Zoom:*

### INDENTURED
By Nancy Stohlman

How much are you getting paid to do this? he asks, a crease in his forehead.

Enough to pay off my student loans, I say, as he begins to tattoo the Coca-Cola logo across my face.

*

*Dialogue and Titles:*

### SOMETIMES THE ONLY RESPONSE IS SILENCE
By Travis Cebula

He pulled a draft of wine nearly as black as his jacket.
"Invented graffiti," he said.
"What?"
"Graffiti. Invented it. 1971."

*

*Experiments with Narrative (backwards):*

### OCEAN NOIR
By Lynn Mundell

He got rid of the gun by hurtling it into the sea, where it sank to the bottom, clanking against the victim's urn, dropped overboard by the cheating widow, who was followed by the jealous detective, who saw her meet the killer at the coffee shop, where trouble always brewed.

*Found Forms:*

## FOR SALE: FAST AND CHEAP
By Paul Beckman

Partial bottles: Beam, Tequila, Peach Schnapps, Gin. Two full cases Bud long necks, half box cigars, X box, golf clubs, take over Fantasy Football team, keg pump, books of chili recipes, assorted beef jerky, fishing crap, beer can and baseball hat collections, girlie mags. Best offer takes all. Husband Convicted.

*

*Bedtime Story:*

## HOTEL KHADIJAH
by Sally Reno

A prostitute of the Hotel Khadijah in Rahab fell in love with my father. Our identity papers were no good there and we couldn't get out, so we had food to eat and a place to sleep then only because of her. I was twice her age so, for the sake of propriety, we said I was Daddy's wife. I would sit in the corridor, in a burqa, in a chair outside the room, while they fucked.

***

When going from flash to microfiction, it can be useful to give yourself a hard constraint to push against. A six-word story is a great place to start. Hemingway's story has been shared so often it's almost a cliché, but just in case you haven't read it:

For Sale: baby shoes, never worn

As with flash, the goal is to write something *as* microfiction rather than just whittling down a longer piece. That said, I have found many of my sculpting exercises (in Part Two), such as cutting a story in half, will often produce a strong microfiction, sometimes even stronger than the original flash. But try different constraints and approaches. Try a 100-word story, then a 50-word story, then a six-word story. See how much you can accomplish in those brief moments when the curtain lifts and reveals your story.

# A Word of Caution: The Biggest Mistake Writers Make

Whether you're writing a story, a poem, a novel, or learning a new genre like flash fiction, the beginning of the writing process should always be play. It's that time of pure inspiration, when your ideas are new and fragile, when risks are taken, mistakes are made, and false starts become discoveries. This creative honeymoon is a time of sweetness and acceptance, a private time between you and your work.

But this is also when your work needs the most protection—it's raw, vulnerable, full of potential, but its wings aren't dry. It's beautiful to us but not ready for the world yet.

These early drafts are about gestation, so it's the worst time to get feedback or be critiqued. The work isn't ready for scrutiny and neither is the author. But we do it anyway: we throw the baby into the pool thinking it can swim; we invite the paparazzi in before we're even dressed. We show the world before we're ready for their reaction, and, like a negative prematurely exposed to the light, our ideas and confidence can fade away in front of our eyes.

And then the writer gives up or gets blocked and doesn't know why.

The biggest mistake writers make is not knowing which stage of the writing process they're in. We confuse writing with editing, we confuse editing with publication, we show work to others before it's ready, we hoard work that *is* ready, afraid of rejection. Realizing which stage of the process you're in—and more importantly what your work needs—is essential.

Wanting to show people your first draft is understandable: you're writing, dammit, and you just want to share it with the world! But a first draft is still growing, and when we thrust our babies into the world too soon, wanting praise or validation, we rarely get it. Not only that, but if the work doesn't outright wither in the spotlights it can go the other direction and become self-conscious, pandering for approval and losing itself.

So don't rush the process. Give yourself privacy. Be unfinished. First drafts need to play and laugh and fail. Let the work figure itself out. Resist bringing in the paparazzi until it can withstand all those flashing lights.

# PART TWO

# SCULPTING FLASH FICTION

# Puberty

And then your baby creation arrives at puberty. This is the true transformation, the metamorphosis, when your work really discovers itself. The child gets stretch marks, rashes of acne, hair in weird places. Sometimes they don't seem like your baby at all— and they're not.

We've arrived at the editing phase, and the honeymoon is over. It's time to change hats: from doting parent to tough love coach. It's time to stop protecting our work. We must be willing to cut it open and lay it all out like a disassembled engine. We must not love it too much at this stage, but we must love it enough to follow through.

This is also when we begin to show our work to an audience. But audience at this stage should be midwives, peers, teachers, and mentors, but only *those you trust*. Those who can tell you that your sunglasses are on your head and likewise point out weaknesses in your work that you've become blind to.

The biggest mistake most writers make in this phase?

Skipping it.

Yes, because we fear this inherently vulnerable process, we can keep our stories hidden like flowers in the dark. But just as you can't skip puberty and go straight from child to adult, these growing pains are necessary for your work to truly mature. Whether it manifests as sweeping revisions or delicate pruning, the editing crucible is where the real magic happens.

I recommend working in a new file. Save that original draft in a separate folder and do the surgery elsewhere, far from the one you love. Take your work by the hand and into the woods for its rite of passage. Let it emerge as a fully formed adult—or not.

# Remodeling: The Endless Possibilities of Revision

*Re-vision.* Literally to see again. During the sculpting process we are re-envisioning our work, looking at it with new and fresh eyes. Revision often stumps writers—they don't know where to begin, or they mistake revision for proofreading. True revision is not about fixing errors. When we revise, we want to pretend as if we've never seen our own work before.

Imagine you're on one of those reality shows where you walk into an empty house with an endless budget and you get to renovate the whole thing according to your vision. It's fun, it's exciting, and everything is full of possibility! And best of all, even if you feel a little nervous about what's ahead, you also know that when you're finished it's going to be MUCH better.

Maybe even…*stunning.*

So embrace the creative invitation of revision: No matter how good that first draft was, it can always get better.

# Trusting Your Reader

One of the hardest (and most important) skills to writing flash is learning to *trust the reader*. As we've said, good flash fiction is a collaboration with the reader—we depend on them to fill in what we purposely leave empty, the silences we allow to ring with meaning. The reader becomes a co-creator in our writing process. We toss them clues, and, like a bloodhound, they follow.

But trusting the reader is tough for many writers. And if you began (as I did) writing long fiction, it can be very counterintuitive. Writers are taught to describe every detail, linger on every passing nuance, dive into every emotion. If we don't write it all out for them, *how will they know?*

They will know if you leave the right clues.

I read a novel recently, a good novel, an acclaimed novel. It had a great storyline and was full of lush, beautiful descriptions. But even though I was invested in the story, I eventually got tired of reading the same lush descriptions over and over, especially for the exact things he'd already described. It made me feel like he didn't trust me to remember, or worse, that he didn't trust himself to have done it right the first time.

Is this a peculiar situation? Nope. This is how writers are taught to write. And I adore lush, lovely descriptions, but there is a huge difference between 100 roses all stuffed together in one vase and the exquisite beauty of a single rose. The single rose takes on a new significance. It becomes the world because it must.

Here in the western U.S., there are beautiful nature hikes through rocky or sandy terrain that do not lend themselves to a clear "path." Instead, the hiker will follow a series of "cairns"—rock pile sculptures—placed at appropriate distances that let them know they're still going the right direction.

Flash fiction is a bit like this. We build a cairn of clues every 20 feet or so, but we also must absolutely trust our readers to find those clues and make the connections. Resist the urge to say it again, just in case they didn't get it the first time. Trust that they are right behind you, keeping up all the way.

# First Impressions: Love at First Sight?

Look at your title—is it the *perfect* title? Is it a love-at-first-sight title? If not, consider it part of your revision process.

There are many kinds of "perfect" titles. I like a title that has actual meaning, when it feels integral and not like an afterthought or pure ornamentation.

Flash writers are discovering what journalists have known all along: headlines and lead sentences—the who-what-when-where-why served up front and without apology—can create clearer communication between writer and reader. If we borrow from journalism (which, incidentally, is another place where writing is often confined by word counts), a flash story can strategically use the title to slip us information even before we have technically started reading.

Because when every word really does count, even the title is an opportunity. It could be used for background or exposition. It could tie the beginning to the end. It could be foreshadowing. Or the title's meaning could change as the story progresses. Maybe the meaning isn't apparent right away, but it's a happy/powerful revelation. Whatever it is, don't waste it.

A title like Ron Carlson's "Bigfoot Stole My Wife," is short and sweet and gives us necessary background information. Longer titles I love include Kona Morris's "I'm Pretty Sure Nicholas Cage is My Gynecologist," Rob Geisen's "The Night I Discovered I Wasn't as Cool as Han Solo," and David S. Atkinson's "Turns Out the Pizza Hut BOOK IT! Program Was Not for Fleeing Tax Evasion Charges."

Notice how each of these titles has a verb?

But a long title isn't the only way to convey essential information and may not be stylistically appropriate. The six-word story below hinges on the title:

### FIRST DATE
By Nick Busheff

At the opera, she chugged beer.

This title is only two words long, but it changes the meaning of everything that follows. Imagine if the title was "At the Opera." What would be lost?

You can also use your title for emphasis, giving yourself the chance to say something twice (an image, an object, a phrase). But make sure this *needs* to be said twice and isn't just a default option. Also consider moving a line. Writer Randall Brown suggests moving the last line of the story into the title role instead, creating a circle from the end back to the beginning. Or, conversely, let the first line become the title, thrusting us into the story *en media res*—or right in the middle of the action.

Whether your title is somber or humorous, long or short, a well-crafted flash fiction title is valuable real estate. It's also your reader's first impression of your story, and falling in love at first sight could be the difference between them reading it...or not.

# Beginnings: Arrive Fashionably Late

I've been to many public readings where the author feels the need to "set the scene" before they read. Sometimes this scene setting takes longer than the piece itself!

When a writer starts setting the scene, I tune out. I don't want to be told what I'm about to see, nor do I want to be told what I missed. I want to press my ear to the door of literature and figure it out myself.

In order to avoid this phenomenon on the page, get to the good part as quickly as possible. This usually means taking a healthy cut at the beginning. The beginning of a story is often like the runway that got the plane into the air, but once you're airborne you don't need it. This can be bittersweet, because, ironically, it's often the image or line that got the whole story started in the first place!

With some courageous excavation you may discover the story really begins two paragraphs later. Think of this like arriving at a party fashionably late. And, as you scrutinize your beginning, always ask the essential flash fiction question: why is this story necessary? Instead of a lot of preamble, scene setting, and throat clearing, identify where the urgency of your story begins and make *that* the first sentence.

# The End

Many writers, even those who begin beautifully, struggle with endings. How many of us were taught in school that a "conclusion" is just a wrapping up, a clever regurgitation of everything already said? Brilliant endings, if they were discussed at all, were held at a distance like sorcery, admired but not imitated.

A brilliant ending should make you go *whoa*. And reread. And go *whoa* again.

Whoa can mean a lot of things: whoa—how messed up, or whoa—how poignant, or whoa—how surprising, or whoa—how perfect. But regardless, it should punch you in the heart or the gut or the head or maybe several places at once. And even if it's just a little punch it should still leave a mark.

Beginnings and endings are like bookends—all the care taken to hook a reader into a story must now cast them out—shaken and forever changed. And this is especially true in flash fiction, where a reader is going from beginning to end in one sitting.

Endings used to be a huge struggle for me. I'd conceive, craft and execute a compelling story, and then I'd tack on a "bow" at the end. In graduate school, I had a professor, Danielle Dutton, who made us examine our beginnings, middles, and endings.

We first examined our openings: how we caught the reader's attention. Then we examined our middles: how we kept the tension pulsing. And then, just as we were getting ready to examine our endings, she threw a wrench in the whole plan and made this suggestion: what if the middle IS the end?

With great discomfort, we turned back to our stories: what if this juicy middle thing I just wrote while under the auspices that I still had more time to "tie it all up" is really the end? What if there is no need for that clever bow, that concluding paragraph... what if it's just...done?

Because that's how it happens in real life anyway, isn't it?

Most writers either over or underwrite their endings. If you are *overwriting* your ending, then chances are the final ringing note of your story is actually buried in the territory of what you're now calling the middle. If you are *underwriting* your ending, it probably means the most crucial part of the story arc still hasn't happened yet—the story isn't done. In that case it's about turning the knife just one more time and seeing what else happens.

The good news about endings is that the work is often just excavating and shaping—and realizing the perfect ending may already be there, fully formed, right in front of your eyes.

# Cliffhangers and Punchlines

Cliffhangers work for television soap operas. Punchlines are perfect for jokes. Neither makes a great ending to a flash fiction story.

# An Inoculation Against Clichés

Writers fear the word "cliché" like it's catching, a sort of literary herpes. And the problem with clichés is that we're surrounded by them—in speech, on television and movies, on billboards. Clichés are the currency of communication, the emoticon of speech. Therefore they can be hard to disentangle from the air we breathe.

Fun fact: the word cliché began with the printing press. In those days, when you wanted to create a page of text, you had to assemble it letter by letter. Words or phrases that were used a lot started to come pre-assembled to save time. These pre-assembled stereotype blocks were called "clichés."

Sayings and slang are one type of cliché. We might think, "On a dark and stormy night" or "happily ever after." The first guy who said, "It's raining cats and dogs" must have seemed like a genius. But when you hear that phrase now, you don't *picture* the dogs, the cats, the sounds of their furry bodies smacking the ground. And that's the problem. If good writing intends our readers to engage, then clichés encourage us to disengage.

Some clichés are so insidious we may not recognize them at first: descriptions like a "pounding heart," characters that are all good or all bad, or storylines that unfold/resolve in predicable ways, like the butler did it or waking from a dream at the end of a story.

In fact, any overworn idea can eventually become a cliché. I once had an early reader tell me that all my characters rolled their eyes. Not believing her, I did a search through my manuscript and found over 100 instances! Needless to say (cliché!) I have not had a character roll their eyes since.

The sin isn't in writing clichés, the sin is in not revising them. Each mindless cliché is an opportunity to say it in your own, unique, fresh, fantastic way. And that's the real problem with clichés—they aren't your original creative wonderful fresh brilliance but a mosaic of everyone else's rehashed ideas. You don't want your readers to disengage from your writing because it's been said a million times (cliché), you want them to be on the edge of their seats (cliché). But if you're using predictable combinations of words in predictable ways, or writing about predictable situations, then your reader is more likely to tune out (cliché) rather than tune in, because he or she has already "been there, done that" (cliché). See?

So here's my favorite technique to inoculate yourself against clichés:

Step away from your editing for one hour and write a story using as many clichés as possible. Cliché phrases, ideas, concepts, idioms, characters, descriptions—really do it up. This will be liberating and fun and ridiculous.

Then after an hour, return to your editing and watch all your own clichés pop right off the page.

# Sculpting Prose: Seeing with the Master's Eye

I was lucky to be part of a weekly workshopping group that met for almost a decade—I call it my "other MFA." Each week we brought our work to the group and got feedback about where we needed "more." More dialogue. More character development. More description. And then we'd all go back to our desks and figure out how to expand.

But, as I started going short, I began to ask a different question: *"What can be taken away?"*

Michelangelo said about his famous statue, *David*: "I saw the angel in the marble and carved until I set him free." Often when we're sculpting our flash fiction it's about clearing away the excess and "finding" the story, learning how to uncover it, prune it, get rid of the bramble.

Now that doesn't mean you can't elaborate on an image or take a longer beat in the story or even add more to clarify. What it does mean is, when confronted with a problem area, your first instinct for adding "more" could become: "What can I get rid of?"

Your editing tool is the scalpel and (sometimes) the machete! Use them to carve and shape and sculpt and even chop, exposing lines, splitting paragraphs, and delicately trimming the excess. Approach your work with curiosity, like a David trapped in a block of marble, and trust that the story sits, fully formed, waiting to be released.

# Shrinking Your Text

Learning how to shrink your text is particularly important to flash. I like to distinguish between two methods: Chipping and Chopping.

Chipping—dehydrating, pruning, carving, sculpting, shaving, scalpel-ing—is when you're removing single words, phrases, perhaps even sentences.

Chopping is when you get rid of whole "sections"— the beginning or the end is common but definitely middles, backstory, whole paragraphs, etc.

How do you know if your story needs chipping or chopping?

Often when someone has a story that is "too long" for flash and they're trying to shrink it, they begin by chipping—taking out words, phrases, and shrinking mostly at the level of the sentences. This feels "safer" at first, but sometimes the result can feel whittled and moth-eaten.

What usually needs to happen, but takes more courage, is a well-placed chop. When chopping, it's less important to pay attention to what's being eliminated and more on *what remains*. You're trying to figure out how to remove the excess so that what remains takes on a new significance.

Chipping, on the other hand, is most effective when your story is well defined overall but feels "wordy." At that point, taking a scalpel and carving at the level of the sentence can make a bloated story feel nice and tight.

Either way, when shrinking your text, the question to ask regardless of whether you're chipping or chopping is: does the reader really *need* this? Will they be confused without it? Will the meaning be changed if I take it out (and do I like the change?).

# Magic Trick: Cut It in Half

Writers aren't always sure what is and isn't necessary in their work, especially since they've lovingly crafted every word. Each story will ultimately tell you what it needs, but a great exercise to make that clearer is to cut your story in half. (Pause for protests…!) Yes—cut it in half. If it's 700 words cut it to 350. If it's 100 words cut it to 50. And then, if you are brave, cut it in half again. You don't need to keep the new version (although often people like the new version(s) better) but it WILL clarify whether your story needs a chip or a chop. Or both. And in some cases you will end up with two (or more) stories that stand equally well.

Observe:

### DEATH ROW HUGGER
#### By Nancy Stohlman
#### [238 words]

For some reason it's always at night. It's always in the same room, the light is always jaundiced. The room smells musty, like wet clothes were shoved and left to die in all the corners.

I guess I was destined for this job. My parents weren't the hugging type, so I've always had a malnourished craving for arms around me. I started out as a professional baby cuddler for the preemie babies in the NICU; each night after visiting hours, I settled into the wooden rocking chair with these miniature babies and their ancient, sculpted faces and whispered of a future when they would be strong and full sized.

But nothing could prepare me for being a Volunteer Hugger on Death Row. You enter that holding room, and there they are, trying to enjoy their steaks or lobsters or Cuban cigars or whatever. My job is to hug them just before they take that long walk. It's not a sexual hug, though I have felt a few erections, and a few have tried to kiss me, but I politely turn my cheek and squeeze them harder. Because there's this moment in the hug, you see, where it goes from something awkward and obligatory to when they melt into my arms, weeping with their bodies if not with their eyes. Every now and then I hear one of them whisper in my ear, and once one called me Mama.

[127 words]

It's always at night. The light is always jaundiced. The room smells musty, like wet clothes were shoved and left to die in all the corners.

I guess I was destined for this job. My parents weren't the hugging type, so I've always craved arms around me.

But nothing could prepare me for being a Volunteer Hugger on Death Row. There they are, trying to enjoy their steaks or lobsters or Cuban cigars or whatever. And there's this moment in the hug, you see, where it goes from something awkward and obligatory to when they melt into my arms, weeping with their bodies if not with their eyes. Every now and then I hear one of them whisper in my ear, and once one called me Mama.

[67 words]

It's always at night. The light is always jaundiced. The room smells musty, like wet clothes were shoved and left to die in all the corners. There they are, trying to enjoy their steaks or lobsters or Cuban cigars. And there's this moment in the hug where it goes from something awkward and obligatory to when they melt into my arms, weeping. Once one called me Mama.

# Swapping

Keeping the mind and the text nimble and fluid is the key to swapping. As soon as we become too attached to one way, we cannot see others.

Often when we have pain in our physical body it's because the fascia, or connective tissue, is actually stuck to the muscle. Whole groups of muscles can get stuck together, and the longer they stay that way, the harder it is to separate them. In a similar way, sometimes the "pain" we feel when editing is because ideas have become stuck together and aren't able to move freely.

Just as chipping and especially chopping will often "reveal" the best lines by exposing them, so, too, does swapping. When you're swapping, you want to look at your story as chunks—particularly sentences and paragraphs—that are separate and mobile, like Legos.

Once you see them as interchangeable parts, start scrambling them.

Within the paragraph, you can try moving around the sentences, particularly in the coveted first and last position. The same for paragraphs as units—try swapping them. I often find a second or third paragraph makes a better first paragraph, and sometimes a paragraph that comes near the end makes a powerful opening.

The goal is to keep your writing loose, keep it malleable like a stick of softened butter that can be shaped and then reshaped.

Like this:

The goal is to keep your writing loose, keep it malleable like a stick of softened butter that can be shaped and then reshaped.

Just as chipping and especially chopping will often "reveal" the best lines by exposing them, so, too, does swapping.

When you're swapping, you want to see your story as chunks—particularly sentences and paragraphs—that are separate and mobile, like Legos. Once you see them as interchangeable parts, scramble them.

Within the paragraph, you can try moving around the sentences, particularly in the coveted first and last position. The same for paragraphs as units—try swapping them. I often find a second or third paragraph makes a better first paragraph, and sometimes a paragraph that comes near the end makes a powerful opening.

Keeping the mind and the text nimble and fluid is the key to swapping. As soon as we become too attached to one way, we cannot see others.

# Juxtapositions and White Space

Vincent Van Gogh understood juxtaposition. He knew that putting yellow next to purple makes the yellow—*yellower* and the purple—*purpler.*

When in the sculpting phase, always look for opportunities to create implication through juxtaposition: word against word, image against image, paragraph against paragraph, and ultimately story against story (in a collection). If done right, the individual pieces are infused with additional meaning simply as a result of their proximity to one another. It's not just the words but the space between and around the word that gives it definition.

This is true for white space on the page, on the canvas, even between the shards of glass in a mosaic. From a distance, impressionist paintings seem full of movement: a whir and blur of color and light and breezes blowing through. Yet up close to the canvas you see the impossible—they're only tiny splotches of color placed next to one another and surrounded by white space!

So pay attention to where you're breaking your sentences and paragraphs, where you're strategically leaving white space between your thoughts. Like nerve endings jumping a synapse, your work should have an electric current that runs from word to word, sentence to sentence, paragraph to paragraph. It's that negative space between the splotches, the well-placed word or phrase vibrating beside but not touching the next, that allows each to breathe and come to life.

# Erasure: Loaded Silences and Intentional Ghosts

Can you remember the last time you experienced an uncomfortable silence? Silences can be full of meaning. What *isn't* said is just as important—and often louder—than what is.

Think of the drama of a full stop in music, the heightened pleasure and payoff of the returning beat. Orchestras stop completely between symphonic movements and everyone sits, rapt, in the loaded silence. When I teach performance, I remind my students to

*pause...*

... because a pause is a way to emphasize what just happened.

Or

a pause can shift a mood     to prepare for what is coming.

The same is true on the page. What isn't said says a lot.

Strategic cutting will activate the power of silences, create gaps of information, and leave purposeful ghosts. And here's the brilliant thing about erasure:

it's like removing a bay leaf from the soup—the flavor remains long after the leaf is gone. Whatever you remove from your work is still there, flavoring the text.

# A Thin Line: Implication vs Confusion

Remember the two rules of flash fiction: it's short—but it also tells a story. Much of our sculpting work so far has assumed that the story is intact and just needs shaping. But there are also drafts with the opposite issue: the writing is tight, condensed and compact—but when it's over we're left baffled, thinking: those were lovely sentences, but I have *no idea what that story was about.*

In this situation there are usually two culprits: 1. there's no story, or 2. there *is* a story, but the writer is using too much implication. While flash fiction loves to subvert the traditional narrative arc and twist, flip, shrink and erase whole chunks of it, there's a thin line between implication and confusion—and it's easy to cross. You don't want the reader to follow your breadcrumbs into the forest and end up lost.

Of course, a certain amount of mystery is fine and even desirable. But picture this: you're reading a story about a woman crying and how her grief feels like rain dripping from leaves. But the story is *supposed* to be about a woman whose dead husband has just been shipped home from the war and she just met his mistress.

You mean that wasn't obvious?

Unfortunately, no. In this case there IS a story, but not enough clues have made it out of the writer's head and onto the page.

If you find yourself in this situation, decide how close you are to revealing the actual story. Will it take just a few key details—a few descriptions of the funeral home, a mention of the military uniform, the mistress standing with a bouquet of roses, etc.—or does the story need more substantial additions? You may need to crack open a scene, expand the dialogue, or let a moment go on longer or deeper. Sometimes you will need to add a whole new section. A helpful question to ask yourself is: what comes *between* these two sentences? What comes between these two paragraphs? Like laying insulation in a drafty house, you discover the cracks, then fill them in. Thankfully stories that fall in this category tend to be short—even ultra short—already, so there's usually plenty of wiggle room.

But, if you're realizing you don't really have a story (yet), if you're still in the realm of character study or scene setting, then you may need to try it from a completely different angle. Remember: something has to happen (on stage or off) to make it a story. Scrutinize your idea for movement and urgency, and if your first attempts still aren't hitting the mark, then

I recommend the method on the next page, which is also a great way to retain one consistent voice throughout a text.

# Flash from Scratch

Sometimes we have nitpicked and tinkered our work to death and it still isn't right. Anaïs Nin says, "Intensive correcting may lead to monotony, to working on dead matter, whereas continuing to write and to write until perfection is achieved through repetition is a way to elude this monotony, to avoid performing an autopsy."

Once our editing starts to feel like an autopsy, like a Frankenstein of parts stuck together (particularly if we've been working on it for a long time), then the best and quickest way to tackle revision is to *write it over, from scratch, without looking.*

If that sounds like a huge waste of time, then be grateful you're writing flash fiction! I give this same advice to all writers, and I myself have rewritten entire novels from scratch. For real.

Rewriting without looking, while initially infuriating, works wonders, especially if you're stuck. Why? Because all the good stuff from that first draft *will* make it into the second draft. And all the mediocre stuff will improve in the rewrite. Almost magically.

Consider how it works in the visual arts. There are often dozens of pre-sketches, studies, and "running starts" at an idea, maybe second, third and fourth versions of a famous painting. In the Dali museum there are multiple renditions of the melting clocks, for instance—dozens of attempts on dozens of canvases until he hit on the famous version we recognize.

I remember the first time I had to rewrite without looking. I had a teacher in college who had us compose drafts by hand in class...then at the end of the class we had to rip those pages out of our notebooks, turn them in, go home, and write it over again!

What?!!

But, because we had no choice, we would all go home and rewrite our drafts from scratch. And the second version was almost always better. Once we quit resisting the process, we discovered that the rewritten drafts were an organic improvement, a maturation of our original ideas, containing all the best parts of the first draft and automatically improving all the weaknesses.

This process works especially well for flash because you can usually rewrite a draft in one sitting. But the process works for everything—poems, novel chapters, scenes, essays. Jack Kerouac rewrote his book *On the Road* from scratch three times. A photographer will shoot the same subject hundreds of times to get just one perfect shot.

And as a bonus, when rewritten all at once, the narrative voice of a story will have a natural cohesion, something that may have been missing in a previous version, particularly if it was composed over a long stretch of time or at various intervals.

When Hemingway was asked why he rewrote the ending to *A Farewell to Arms* 39 times, he said, "To get the words right." So, for this reason, I suggest closing that document, open a new one, and write it again. The effort will be worth it.

# On Creating Distance from Your Text

Lastly, when you're in the editing phase, you must find a way to create distance from your text. It can be hard to see your work with fresh eyes—like looking for your sunglasses when they're on your head. The best way to create distance, of course, *is actual distance.* There's nothing more revealing than a month away from your work. But there are other ways to create distance from your story if you don't have the luxury of time.

*Read it out loud.* When you use your ear rather than your eye you can "hear" when the rhythm is off. If you stumble over a word in your spoken delivery, chances are that word is awkwardly placed. If you cut or add words in the spoken delivery, cut or add them on the page. If you find yourself amending the text as you read it, pay attention to those clues.

*Change the font.* Something as simple as a font change can refresh how we "see" our work. (This also goes for colors and backgrounds.)

*Print it out.* Just as changing the font allows you to "see" your words differently, printing it out and holding it in your hand will also change the dynamic.

Once printed, read it from beginning to end as quickly as possible, making notes about what strikes you but not stopping to linger.

*Read it backwards.* Not word for word but go backwards in chunks. This is especially helpful when you are "swapping." Notice what happens when you read it backwards—particularly how endings or potential endings land or jump out at you. Usually the perfect ending for your story or manuscript is already in there, buried. Watch your sentences come unglued in the best way.

# A Word of Caution: Flashlights

Remember: all edits should be in service of the story. A good editor can shine a flashlight into the cracks, give suggestions, help brainstorm, and be a sounding board, but in the end it's your story and you always know what serves your story best.

That said, you should pay close attention to two kinds of feedback: the kind you instantly agree with and the kind you instantly reject.

When a piece of feedback resonates, you'll get an immediate "a-ha!" Follow those impulses—they may (and usually do) lead to breakthroughs. It doesn't mean that the feedback itself is the answer, but it means the flashlight is pointing down the right path.

On the other hand, another piece of feedback will be hard to hear. Assuming the feedback was given in a constructive way by a person who wants your story to succeed (never underestimate that part!), then it's probably also shining a light into a blind spot or exposing a weakness that needs to be explored.

Once you begin the editing process, also beware of extreme reactions: taking every bit of feedback in order to "please" the editor (and losing touch with your story), or rejecting good feedback before discovering if there might be a flashlight in there for you. I always suggest marinating in feedback for at least a day or two (a week, a month—the bigger the piece the longer you should wait!) because sometimes it takes a while to digest new information and uncover how those new pathways might unfold.

But the bottom line: you are in service of the story. You are the midwife of the story. It's not about making an editor happy. It's about making *the story* happy.

# PART THREE

# FLASH FICTION BOOKS

# The Big Picture: Micro to Macro

Flash fiction has naturally inspired books, including flash anthologies, flash collections, novellas-in-flash and flash novels. Some of these forms are familiar, and some are still soft and pliable. Whether you're an editor working on an anthology, an author assembling a collection, or you're embarking on a hybrid, flash fiction-inspired novel or novella, you need different tools and strategies when you shift from the micro to the macro view of a body of work.

# On Printing Things Out

In this digital world, printing out your work can seem like a waste of time and paper. Print it out anyway. Let the process be physical. I assure you, particularly when envisioning a large-scale project like a book, it changes your perspective when you hold it in your hands.

Printed work can also be physically manipulated in the real world. This allows for the wisdom and intuition of the body as part of your ordering (or revision) process: *seeing* the pieces (not just on a screen), *feeling* what happens when you move them around or tape them to your walls, *listening* to how the stories brush up against each other and what kind of neighbors they make. It becomes a tangible experience. It's the difference between playing solitaire online and shuffling a real deck of 52 cards in your hands.

# The Great Shuffle: Anthology or Collection?

Let's get our terminology straight. By anthology I mean a book of stories written by many different authors; the editor conceives, solicits, judges, and orders the pieces into the final product. By collection I mean a book that features the work of just one author, usually put together by that author.

What is required is very different.

Ordering an anthology is like taking a 3rd grade class photo: everyone needs to be in the picture. You might have pieces that are wildly different. You might have four kids all wearing green sweaters. Your job is to make everyone look good. Whether you decide to put all the tall kids in the back or alternate by sweater color, you're working with a lot of disparate pieces and are limited by your materials—your challenge is to arrange them in the most interesting and pleasing order, showcasing each while creating a cohesive whole.

Ordering a collection—especially your own collection—is much different. There's a new power available in a collection—you don't just have artistic license over the order—you have artistic license over *the whole thing*. Now there's the possibility of manipulating, even rewriting stories as you build that cohesive whole—a cardinal sin in an anthology.

Even readers treat them differently. Anthology readers have no qualms about reading the stories out of order—in fact, we almost expect them to go straight for the Table of Contents and look for their favorite authors. But the reader of a collection will often read the stories in order, and in this way a collection must behave like a novel, *enticing* the reader to keep turning pages and finding something fresh on each one.

So whether you're working on a collection or an anthology, consider the act of ordering to be a crucial part of the creative process. Writers who are too quick to "get the ordering over with" miss a lot of untapped potential. Solving the puzzle of arranging is just as essential, deliberate, and nuanced as the writing itself. And just as revealing.

# Curation vs Creation

Stepping into the role of an editor is extremely useful to understanding the process of ordering. As the editor of an anthology (or journal), your job is curation. A truly inspired editor is creating more than just a container for multiple stories. You're often working with a variety of styles, lengths, rhythms, themes, and subjects that can be wildly different from one another. Your task is to produce a satisfying journey through these diverse pieces, a whole that feels greater than the sum of its parts.

Art exhibits—which are also journeys through artifacts purposely arranged—are great examples of inspired curation. Recall a favorite art or museum exhibit: how was it arranged? Were the artifacts clumped by similarities? Sizes? Interspersed by color and theme? Did you follow a journey or narrative? A chronology? Or even something unconventional?

There is no "right" way to curate, and given 10 artifacts you could arrange them in many different ways. The choices you make are part of your style. Some editors might put the most famous authors first or in some other place of honor. Another editor might chunk or intersperse the stories by theme, style, tone, or point of view. One Fast Forward anthology, *The Incredible Shrinking Story,* arranged stories in descending order from longest to shortest. Then again, another writer I know says she drops all her stories on the floor, picks them back up, and that's the order. Try them all, lest we take ourselves too seriously.

# Japanese Flower Arranging

In Japan there is a long tradition of ikebana, or the art of flower arranging, which, according to the Ikebana International website, is "more than simply putting flowers in a container." They define ikebana as "a disciplined art form in which the arrangement is a living thing where nature and humanity are brought together…its heart is the beauty resulting from color combinations, natural shapes, graceful lines, and the meaning latent in the total form of the arrangement."

I particularly like the idea of an arrangement as a "living thing" that allows for "latent meaning" to come through. And I love the way this aesthetic relates to curation: one story humming against the next *will* inform how you read them both, buzzing with subtext and unspoken potential.

# The Concert Setlist

Another way to think about curation is the concert setlist. When I edited *Fast Forward: The Mix Tape*, I channeled my most favorite experience of arranging: making a 1980's era "mixed tape."

From my introduction to that book: "I wrote each of the stories on a flash card…and spread the stories over every inch of my living room as I would have my music long ago. Funny the patterns that started emerging, like beetles, cockroaches, cheese, Jesus… an apocalyptic pizza parlor spread out before me. Stylistic themes emerged, too, stories told in one long breathless sentence, stories told through numbered lists, ultra-flash stories (under 100 words)."

In this way, your Table of Contents is your concert setlist—should you open the show with a hit song? A mellow song and then work up to a hit song? A fast song? A brand new song? End with the biggest song? End on something poignant? End on a ballad? Should you break up the familiar songs with a cover song? You might not put two ballads together, but too many rocking songs in a row could start sounding the same, losing their individuality and diluting the effect.

Study the Tables of Contents from several published anthologies and notice those editors' choices around curation, including *length* (short, medium, long), *narrator* (female or male, child or adult or other), *point of view* (1st, 2nd, or 3rd), *style* (humorous, dramatic), *reoccurring themes or imagery* (mothers, babies, fathers, relationships, childhood, food, dreams, absurdity) and others.

Now reorder their stories in several different patterns. Pay particular attention to first lines and last lines: how does the last line of one story feel vibrating against the first line of the next? Imagine the first and last stories as a circle—how would they feel if they were connected?

# Happy Little Accidents

In any artistic project, it's also important to embrace the unexpected, the accidental, and the random. In the words of Bob Ross, we should have "happy little accidents." Especially in the early stages of a big work, you should resist getting too attached to one idea. We want to keep the clay soft and shapeable for as long as possible.

Why? Because as soon as a writer knows everything about her book, it gets boring. In fact, that's usually the reason a writer quits a project—it's no longer interesting. It no longer holds any mystery or surprise. And trust me, if a writer is bored with their work, a reader will be, too.

So allow for delightful surprises and beautiful randomness.

Try this: put all your stories in a metaphorical (or a real) hat, shake them up, toss them all in the air and let them land on the metaphorical floor. Notice what you notice. Do two stories "land" next to each other that you would never have put together but...look at that! How interesting! Watch how stories begin talking to each other in unexpected ways. Allow for the beauty of randomness to challenge or inform what you thought you knew. Introduce a sense of play and messiness into this process, a sense of curiosity about how it all might shake out. Let the chaos create meaning; let the pieces make new neighbors and spark new *a-has!*

# Making the Cut

Whether you're putting together an anthology or a collection of one person's work—likely your own—you will eventually have to decide who makes the team.

Choosing for an anthology can be easier in once sense because there will be natural variety. And, as a bonus, picking the best from hundreds of choices forces you to get really clear, to ask not only *if* you liked a piece but *why* you liked it, and most importantly, did you like it *enough*? You start to understand at a cellular level whether something works or not. A piece that might be pretty good on its own will show its weaknesses when put alongside 500 others.

On the other hand, you might think choosing for a collection isn't hard: just pick your best ones. And yes, ultimately you pick the best stories. But too often a collection includes everything, because choosing favorites can be painful. Each story is our beloved child and we want them all included.

The bad news: only the very best 30-40% should make it into a book, which means if more than half of your work is making it into the collection, then you're not writing enough.

Another logic is to choose only stories that have been previously published. This also makes good sense—if someone else has published it, it must be good. But remember: especially when choosing for a collection, you aren't just looking for good. You're making an entirely new artifact.

# The Compilation vs the Concept Album

If the anthology is the compilation album, then the single author collection is the concept album. And when you are both the writer of the material and the designer of the book, you have a new level of creative control. As you gather and arrange your own stories, you might discover and fill gaps by writing new material, changing tenses, syncing characters, manipulating narrators, and otherwise matching or contrasting the stories as needed. And the stories may begin to take on second and third layers of subtext–no longer just individuals but the synergy of something much bigger.

That said, it's also entirely possible to approach a collection as you approached the anthology: with the Japanese flower arranging method, the concert setlist, the 3rd grade class photo, and even the beautiful chaos of randomness. But the benefit of curating your own work is there are also more possibilities, a pliability that's available precisely because you are also the *source* of the material. Rather than just a showcase album of all you've done, what *new* story might you tell with these pieces?

# A Word of Caution: Party Tricks

A body of work needs variety and diversity, and that's especially apparent with single author collections. As writers, we all have our quirks and obsessions—they lend to our style, voice, and individuality. But our party tricks can, if not properly arranged, feel like sameness when all gathered under one roof.

What do I mean by party tricks? Any unintentional or reoccurring pattern (usually unconscious) can become a party trick—maybe the final line of every story ends on a dramatic image. Maybe every story begins with the same rhythmic pattern. Maybe the same subject matter is over explored. It's like your writerly "tic."

The most disappointing thing for me when I sit down to a collection is enjoying the first stories, settling into that writer's style and manner, and then never again being *surprised*. The story that may have taken my breath away as a stand-alone will no longer take my breath away if it was preceded by six others exactly like it. The pieces can start to sound alike precisely because the writer has put them all side by side...and unknowingly exposed their own formulas.

Once your reader has discovered your party trick, you better have another. Just when I think I've got you figured out, I want you to have something else up your sleeve.

# Threads: Plucking Patterns

A pattern on purpose, however, is a whole different thing. We're surrounded by patterns, both conscious and unconscious. The patterns in a blanket, a carpet, a doily. The patterns of music or song lyrics. The patterns in a movie—how often and with what regularity do we return to certain themes, story lines, characters.

In the book *Meander, Spiral, Explode,* Jane Alison says: "For centuries there's been one path through fiction we're mostly likely to travel—one we're actually told to follow—and that's the dramatic arc: a situation arises, grows tense, reaches a peak, subsides....And it is an elegant shape, especially when I translate arc to its natural form, a wave....But so many other patterns run through nature, tracing other deep notions of life. Why not draw on them, too?"

Consider the pattern(s) of your book. Does it make a straight line? An oval? Is it orderly like rows of grapes in a vineyard? Does it explode like a Pollock splatter? Mushroom? Rise from the floor like a stalagmite? Does it form, split, and reform? Zigzag up a mountain? Does it race? Take sharp corners? Does it pulse from the center? Whirlpool in circles? Or does it gently bob and float like a leaf swept along a lazy river?

If you had to draw the shape of your book, what would it be?

Now try another shape.

Teasing out the patterns in your work is like weaving a tapestry. The red you throw in now might end up as a bright red zigzag through the whole book. An anthology editor can clump and rearrange, but as the designer of your own collection you can actually *add more red*. Or even a splash of gold.

# Name That Book

Naming a book can be daunting, but it's extremely important. I suggest re-rereading the chapter on titles, as everything there applies here. But one ripe and overlooked source of naming material is the titles of the individual pieces themselves. Test each individual title as a title for the whole book and see if anything clicks.

# Literary Mosaics and the Novella in Flash

Often within a traditional book-length narrative there are many "islands" of story, plus a whole lot of connective tissue getting us from one island to the next. Now imagine a book that's *only the islands:* only the best parts, the juicy parts, full of color and conflict. Or, as Elmore Leonard said in his Ten Rules of Writing: "Try to leave out the part that readers tend to skip."

Halfway between a single-author collection and a flash novel is the slippery creature now being called the novella-in-flash. For our purposes think of this as a longer story told in flash fiction "chapters." This type of work is a natural extension of a threaded collection, but it's a more *deliberate* and more highly planned mosaic composed of self-contained pieces but also meant to stand together as a bigger whole.

A longer story being told through pieces is not new. Consider: Bram Stoker wrote *Dracula* as a series of letters, journal entries, newspaper clippings, doctor's notes, and even a ship's log, among others. The difference, however, between a book like *Dracula,* which is indeed made of pieces, and a novella-in-flash, is that in the latter the pieces are complete and can stand alone.

When considering a novella-in-flash, your scope is both large and small: you're creating a big story made of tiny stories, meant to be appreciated individually and as shards that, when viewed from a distance, make up a larger image.

Writing a novella-in-flash also satisfies multiple urges—the quick payoff of writing flash with the long-term relationship that is writing a novel. You can approach this kind of text in many ways. If you already have a bunch of related flashes, you can pull them aside and start there. But you can also come at it from a completely different angle: taking the big idea and breaking it into pieces as you would break a sheet of glass to create a mosaic.

Think of a story you want to write, a complex story that can't be told in just one flash. Now, *very quickly* write down 100 chapter titles. Don't overthink this—100 chapter titles is a lot so the faster you go the better.

Then begin writing those chapters, in any order. You'll naturally be drawn to some first—start there. And remember—just because a chapter is short does not mean it's flash fiction. Many books have short chapters in order to keep you turning pages. A flash fiction chapter is short but self-contained and tells a story. So, as you write, test each chapter for stand-aloneness *and* put the whole story together for scope and tension.

The more you write the more your list will change—that's ok. The best part of this technique is that, when stuck in your creative process, you can return to your list of titles and just pick another.

# The Flash Novel: Build It and They Will Come

We've arrived at the most protean form: the flash novel.

What's a flash novel?

The flash novel is an impulse born out of flash fiction, an impulse toward brevity, implication, compression, and experimentation. The flash novel is not accidentally short, it's intentionally short. While it may be comprised of flash chapters, it doesn't have to be. The entire book, however, has the urgency and ingenuity of flash fiction.

In this way the flash novel can't really be called a novella even though they may share length. The flash novel is a different beast born out of different intentions: maybe you chop your novel in half. Maybe you zoom or use found forms. Maybe you gather flash pieces into a mosaic. Maybe you thread together a novel-scope concept album.

Plenty of work could be "grandfathered" into this category. Selah Saterstrom's *The Pink Institution* makes use of both threaded, self-contained pieces as well as found forms, including lists and photograph inscriptions. Jenny Offal's book *Dept of Speculation* is composed of hundreds of tiny microfictions but covers the span of a novel. Even Hemingway approaches *Old Man and the Sea* with the zoom lens: focusing on just three days with very little backstory, allowing the narrative to drag us like a giant marlin all the way to the end without even one chapter break.

So, are these flash novels? At just 120 pages, the publisher called *Old Man and the Sea* a "novel" most likely because Hemingway was already famous. Truman Capote's *Breakfast at Tiffany's* is roughly 100 pages and has been called both a novella and a short novel and was originally published alongside three short stories to create a book of 160 pages.

But the 100-page book and the 160-page book are different artifacts with different objectives.

Reading a flash novel is like sitting down to a two-hour movie. Because we travel from the beginning to the end in just one (or a few) sitting, we can see the end approaching even as we begin the journey. While we may read a traditional novel over many days, weeks, or months, the flash novel explodes all at once, giving it an urgency and immediacy not unlike flash fiction.

And, just as flash fiction did not fit into an accepted genre and needed to establish its own legitimacy, the flash novel doesn't currently have its own category. It's not able to "check" any of the submission boxes.

The would-be flash novel of 100 pages may now find itself having to double just to meet industry standards. And...adding unnecessary bulk runs counter to the flash mentality of essentialism. Therefore, just as new territory had to be forged and cultivated for a flash fiction reading audience, so, too, will readers and publishers need to rethink the possibilities of a fiction manuscript to include the complex, creative, and devastating works being created in miniature.

New thought requires new terminology. There's power in naming.

# Conducting the Symphony

A full orchestra has approximately 70-100 wildly different instruments, from the viola to the trombone, the harp to the timpani. What makes a symphony beautiful is the exquisite synergy of all these different pieces. Sometimes the orchestra quiets as the oboe talks. Sometimes the strings play at full mast, layered by the trumpeting of a tuba. Sometimes there's a gong. And what keeps these 100 elements in harmony, working together as a whole? The conductor.

When creating a flash novel (or any other flash book), you are the creator, composer, curator, and conductor of a beautiful symphony. And just like the conductor, you must keep everything together and separate: you need to intimately know each individual piece AND hold a vision of something bigger.

You have all the tools of flash fiction at your fingertips. Maybe you create a threaded flash narrative. Or a breathless book, the novella-in-flash minus the story titles. Or a micro novel. Or something that doesn't exist yet. While the flash novel may still be elusive as we dream this form into being, it also opens new possibilities for a new kind of book. Work that breaks with tradition is never immediately welcomed, but that doesn't make it any less necessary.

# PART FOUR

# GOING SHORT

# Grown Adult Living in the Basement

We've arrived at the final phase of the creative process: the grown adult living in the basement phase. This is when we've worked on something until it's done, but for some reason we can't let it go. Maybe we're afraid to face the daunting wall of rejection. Maybe we're afraid to face the blank page. Maybe the perfectionist in us won't let it go because it's not "perfect."

This is a fearful stage for lots of good reasons. First, there's the very real possibility and (let's be honest) probability of rejection. This creation you've worked so hard on is going to be subjected to, well, everything, as it goes into the world without you. So, like overprotective parents, we might lock it up in the basement "for its own protection."

There's another reason we sit on our work like a Mother Hen—we'd rather stay in the "editing" phase indefinitely than face the finality of finishing. Finishing would mean it's time to face the blank page again, and that's its own kind of scary.

But let it go we must. It's now over gestated, rotting in the womb; we can even ruin it if we stay there too long. Knowing when something is finished is just as important as any other part of the process. All creations have their own cycles, their own lifespans and their own destinies. If we don't release them when they are finished, we miss the moment— the train leaves the station, the soufflé falls. Perhaps it's time to send it out for publication. Perhaps it's a book. And perhaps it goes nowhere and that's okay too. Whatever its destiny, the writer needs to let the work go and move forward—lead it to the ocean, put it in a bottle and set it adrift.

When the child is grown, buy them a suitcase.

# Rejection Is Good

If you aren't getting rejections, then you aren't in the game. If everything you submit gets accepted, it's time to take bigger risks.

While it might be discouraging to hear that our work isn't ready, whether that's a single story or a whole book, it can be the best thing that ever happens to us. Getting that rejection forces us back to the page, back to our work, again and again.

# Not Writing

Not writing is painful. Unfinished work sitting there is painful. You might beat yourself up with a bunch of "shoulds" and berate your lack of discipline. It can make you feel hopeless, drained of energy, and questioning if it's even worth it. No wonder you keep avoiding it!

But there are usually some very good reasons why you're avoiding your work. To start with, you're a better writer now. Just do the math: if you started even one year ago, then you're a better writer now. And that's a good thing! That's the beauty of practice paying off. But it can also feel frustrating when you realize that first story or first draft, the one you labored over, might have made you a better writer but isn't at your level anymore.

Or you're in a different emotional place. Often the impetus that drove us to the page resolves or fades; whatever we were grappling with has been settled. Perhaps we're on the other side of a life change, and the early writing was part of our process, but now we aren't "feeling it."

Or you're overly loyal to your original vision. After all, you've probably put in countless hours of work. But sometimes we become too attached to our original vision; sometimes we've read and reread our sentences so many times we can't imagine them any other way. And when we can't imagine new possibilities for our work, when everything is known and nothing unknown…well, then it's no wonder we're not writing.

And, finally, you might be shifting gears. This almost always happens to me after finishing a big project. After a book, for instance, I consider myself creatively postpartum for at least 6-12 months, recovering from the birth and taking care of the new baby. Anything I try to write in that time will end up sounding exactly like what I was writing before because I'm still in the old mindset.

But, regardless of the reason, it's discouraging to find yourself fallow, quiet. The best thing to do is give yourself a break. The creative process ebbs and flows, and what goes up must go down. Trust the process. Read more. I especially like to reread favorite books in these periods—sink into the familiar and rekindle your love of words. And remember: all creation is ultimately play. Get silly and messy and re-discover what is joyful. Be curious. Be ridiculous. Be shameless. Take a bold risk into new territory and allow yourself to fail. No one has to know.

# How Do You Know When It's Finished?

Writers are often too eager to publish. And yes—it's extremely satisfying to get that official stamp of approval on your work. But...you shouldn't rush to publish until the work is ready.

How do you know when it's ready?

It's different for everyone, but I sit on stories for months. I know a story or book is finished when I can return to it after at least a month away and I don't want to change a thing.

# Publish Small, Then Big

Just as you wouldn't start painting on an 8-foot canvas, you usually need to publish small before you can publish big.

I used to think that publishing my work in small venues would "waste" it. And then I discovered something really important: publication is publication. It means someone enjoyed my work enough to put their stamp on it. And publication makes us feel, well, published. Official. It's far better to start feeling official than to wait for validation from a big venue that you might not be ready for, yet. And, as a bonus, it's much easier to get published once you've been published.

Luckily there's an entire world of small publications and electronic magazines out there, and provided you did a solid job of writing and editing, there will likely be a home for your work. Seek out journals that are just starting out—they'll be more actively looking for new work. Also consider themed issues—sometimes a funky story that has a hard time getting published alone will be just perfect for a themed issue. Submitting to contests alone can be a mixed strategy until you have some publication momentum, as they will all charge a fee and your chances of winning will be slimmer. Instead, watch where other flash fiction writers are getting published and read those journals—they're probably run by cool writers who just might become your colleagues.

# Skin in the Game

Most writers don't like to hear that they'll need to write a few "practice books." I personally have three practice books, and it's a mercy I was too poor to even consider self-publishing, because I understand the temptation to just *get it out there.* It was a blessing I didn't have that option because my work wasn't ready.

Here's the thing about self-publishing: writers used to have to work very hard to get a book published. You'd really have to go "through the fire." And that fire, including all those rejections, was part of the alchemy that made great writers out of good writers.

That doesn't mean that good work isn't self-published or that big publishers don't publish bad books. It just means there are a lot of books out there that aren't ready. It's now become possible to publish a book without ever *getting a single rejection.*

But, even more concerning for authors, self-publishing has created a loophole where a publisher gets paid whether your book sells or not, leaving authors and their books orphaned, often without the necessary skills to find their readership. Self-publishers are all too happy to take your money and give you a "product" without putting any skin in the game. A lawyer who doesn't get paid unless she wins will be sure to win. A publisher who doesn't get paid if your book doesn't sell will make sure your book sells.

# Why Self-Promotion Is Not Shameless

Do you hate the idea of self-promotion? Do you tell yourself that you're not good at it? That you shouldn't have to do it? Do you apologize every time you do it? If you hate self-promotion, or even the prospect of self-promotion, you're not alone. Many artists share a similar aversion: we just want to be left alone with our work and let someone else handle the promotion part. Most of us are waiting for an agent/manager/ publicist to come and rescue us from the prospect of having to promote...*ourselves*?

But *why*?

As artists, we've internalized certain agreed-upon stories, certain cultural mythologies that may be blocking our ability to put ourselves and our work into the world. But the catch is: if we want to be taken seriously, we have to start playing seriously. So it's worth taking a look at these stories and deciding whether perpetuating them is serving our careers— or not.

THE STARVING ARTIST STORY: "I'M NOT GOING TO
MAKE ANY MONEY AT THIS, ANYWAY."

If we were running a company, a large portion
of our budget would go to marketing, right? If we
were selling shoes, our livelihood would depend on
us getting out there and selling some shoes. Even
if we were running a lemonade stand, we would
understand that, in order to sell lemonade, we'd need
to make signs or recruit neighborhood kids with
megaphones to let people know that *lemonade is
available*. If no one knows about our lemonade, then
no one will buy it no matter how fantastic it might be.

But when it comes to our art, we've subscribed to
a "starving artist" story that tells us we're probably
not going to make any money at this, anyway, so we
don't take the task of promotion seriously. In fact,
most of us would probably do a better job promoting
the lemonade than the art we've poured our blood
and souls into.

If you want to make a career out of your
art, then you have gone into business—*with
yourself.* My product is my work. If no one knows
about my product, they can't buy it. And then I'm
out of business.

Many of us don't promote because we would
rather fail privately than publicly. We fear rejection
and ridicule; we retreat into craft instead. But if we're

stoking the starving artist story, then we're going into the game already defeated. If we believe we can't make a living from our art…then we probably won't.

## THE OVERNIGHT SUCCESS STORY: "ONCE I'M FAMOUS SOMEONE ELSE WILL DO THIS."

This is the mythical tale of the artist who is catapulted into fame from obscurity with little effort of their own. While this mythology is exciting, and the media loves to dangle it as a strange version of the American Dream, it's also a bit like expecting to win the Powerball.

The overnight success story is a darling of artists and runs deep in our culture. But if you look carefully behind most successes, you will usually find a different story. Madonna made hundreds of demos with her own money and personally brought them to every DJ in New York City; Truman Capote sat for 8 hours a day in the lobby of the publisher who refused to see him. Even Rosa Parks, our favorite little old lady who wouldn't give up her seat on the bus and triggered the Civil Rights Movement, was actually a veteran activist for 15 years when she was finally in the right place at the right time.

Because that's what it comes down to: "It's not enough to be at the right place at the right time—you have to be the right *person* at the right place at the right time," says musical agent Justin Sudds in his interview for "Take Your Talent to the Bank." The truth of the overnight success story is that it's usually not overnight at all.

But the biggest problem with the overnight success story is that we ultimately cede the authority and responsibility for our careers over to someone else. Like playing roulette, we are at the mercy of outside forces, hoping to hit it big while feeling powerless to affect real change. And I like playing roulette, but only with what I am prepared to lose.

"IT'S NOT POLITE TO BRAG."

This is the story that really paralyzes us.

Here's the truth: will some people be annoyed by your promotional efforts? Yes. But usually the ones who are annoyed, offended, or otherwise triggered by your efforts are the ones who have not fully embraced their own. So their support or non-support for you and your work really has little to do with you and more to do with them. It's pretty hard to jump on someone else's bandwagon when your own bandwagon isn't moving. It's pretty hard to muster up enthusiasm for someone else when you haven't really put your own work out there. So when you encounter this kind of resistance: be kind.

But most of the people won't care, and in fact they'll be happy that you've made it so easy for them to support you. It's said that a person needs to hear something five times (yes, five!) before they take action, and in our busy world most people are happy for the reminders.

Bottom line: self-promotion is not bragging. It's asking for the support we need to create the lives we want.

In this puritan society we're told "it's better to give than receive." Most of us have a hard time even admitting what we want, let alone asking for it. But if I want people to read my work—I have to ask. If I want people to come to my website, my lecture, or buy my latest book—I have to ask. You can't fault people if you haven't even asked.

In our everyone-for-himself society we've attached a stigma to asking for help. But we also have to remember that artists must exist in community, and you have to put yourself out there with honesty and authenticity. Self-promotion is about asking for the support we need and building relationships with those who are excited about us and our work. IT'S THE GREATEST THING YOU CAN DO FOR THE PROMOTION OF ART OUTSIDE OF CREATING THE ART ITSELF.

And yes, it's true that Emily Dickinson did no promotion. But then again, she never got to enjoy the rewards, respect, or recognition of her work while she was alive.

I want more for myself and my art.

And I want more for you, too.

# Not a Dirty Word: Self-Promotion Advice for Writers

WRITE A GOOD BIO. This one should be easy—but writing a bio is often the first resistance. If you find yourself saying, "I don't like to praise myself," then I ask you this: if you can't praise your work, how do you expect anyone else to? Find that balance between impressive and humble; be professional while still reflecting your writerly personality. Read lots of other bios and make note of the ones that stay with you. First impressions are important, and your bio is often the first contact a potential reader has with you.

TAKE A REAL PICTURE. Don't just crop your face from the group New Year's Eve shots. You probably know someone who knows someone who is dabbling in photography—do a little bartering. Buy them lunch in exchange for a subject to practice on. Again, it's all about first impressions: your potential reader will only take you as seriously as you take yourself.

HAVE A WEBSITE. Social media alone doesn't count. People who are (or will be) looking you up need to land on a real website: one concise place where they can read your bio, see your picture, read your list of publications, and purchase your work.

You don't have to spend a lot of money on this. There are plenty of inexpensive or even free blogging and hosting sites, and if later you want to upgrade, you can.

PUBLISH STUFF. This kind of goes without saying, but you'd be surprised how many writers guard their work as if it can only be published in one holy glob—and that ultimately puts them in a position of trying to publish an entire book with few other publishing credits. The best way to get people excited about your work is to let them read it. It's impossible to be excited about your work if it's guarded away. So publish stories, offer to guest blog or write book reviews for your colleagues—but publish stuff. I aim to publish 12 pieces a year—which means I send out at least three times that many.

THOU SHALT NOT PROMOTE BY INTERNET ALONE. Get out of the house! Be part of the community—try reading your work at literary events in your town. Can't find a literary event in your town? Start one. Some of my earliest public appearances were "salons" held in people's living rooms. Invite some other writers, bring some wine, and you've just created a literary event that may grow legs and become a vortex of community.

SUPPORT OTHER WRITERS. You may worry that there aren't enough publishers or readers, and that every other writer's success is a threat to yours. But that's just not true—there's plenty for everyone, and the best way to get the flow coming back to you is to send it out to others. Applause is contagious. So openly support the work and promotional efforts of your colleagues, honor those who've paved the way before you, and commit to sharing your successes with those who follow.

Together, let's tell a new story.

# THE FLASH REVOLUTION

## The Story Is Dead! Long Live the Story!

When the world changes, art must change. Artists must say what needs to be said in a new and vital way. But artistic movements are rarely welcomed—they're almost always dismissed as vulgar and simplistic and worse: not real art.

Writer and filmmaker Alain Robbe-Grillet, one of the leaders of the French New Wave, sums it up: "A new form will always seem more or less an absence of any form at all, since it is unconsciously judged by reference to the consecrated forms....This stammering newborn work will always be regarded as a monster, even by those who find experiment fascinating."

And we've seen it time and again. The Impressionists tried to have an art showing in France in 1873—their request was denied. The public was horrified by Beethoven's Ninth Symphony, now considered his masterpiece, because he had added a choir—a choir!—in the final "Ode to Joy." Stravinsky was practically run out of town at the debut of *The Rite of Spring* as people rioted in the streets. Rock n' roll records were publicly burned in giant bonfires while racist preachers warned teens that Satan had arrived.

Literature isn't immune. The "novel" was once considered trashy, commonplace, and only good for women! And imagine the debut of free-verse poetry! Walt Whitman's *Leaves of Grass* was ridiculed for breaking every rule of good poetic taste in 1855, but it opened the door to what *had never been possible before.*

Artistic movements happen because they're needed—the old ways no longer suffice. According to Mark Rothko, abstract expressionism emerged after WWII because painters needed to say something *that had never been said before.* Selah Saterstrom calls this "growing a new tongue."

Writers are changing. Readers are changing. The world is changing and therefore literature is changing. Flash fiction answers a call, acts against convention, creates a new form for a new world.

James Thomas says, "It's hard to know whether fifteen years ago writers weren't writing these stories or editors simply weren't accepting them for publication, but I'm inclined to think (as both an editor and a writer at that time) that editors were… considering them 'slight' if not whimsical."

But we know flash fiction is anything but slight, and those assumptions are full of unexamined ideas, including small must be easy, important must be big, and no one has any capacity for attention. We know tiny is part of the art.

To be part of an emerging genre is a privilege that doesn't come in every lifetime. The form is still soft and pliable. No one else is telling us how to write flash (yet). We are leading this movement—we are the innovators and the visionaries. So we must surrender to the work, get out of the way, and write what wants to be written. The best ideas rarely fit into neat check boxes.

# APPENDIX

## 100 (FlashNano) Prompts

1. Write a story in which something transforms into something else.
2. Write a true story that no one would believe.
3. Find a story you've written that isn't quite working. Chop it down to exactly 100 words. Give it a new title.
4. Write a story that is based in or uses elements of mythology—any mythology from any culture or time period.
5. Bibliomancy—open the dictionary to any random page, place your finger on any random word and poof! That is the title (or part of the title) of your next story.
6. Write a story from the point of view of someone much older than you.
7. Write a story about or featuring a body part.
8. Write a story in which something important is lost.
9. Use a dream or pieces of a dream to create a surreal story.

10. Find a story of yours that's not quite working. WITHOUT rereading it, rewrite it from scratch.
11. Write a story that begins with, and consists mostly of, dialogue.
12. Write a story that deals with or includes some aspect of a taboo.
13. Write a story that has happened to you, but write it from another person's point of view.
14. Write a story that involves a reoccurring and/or deep dark fear.
15. Write a story that happened to someone else, but write it as if it happened to you.
16. Write a story that has some reference to a current event.
17. Write a story that involves an animal.
18. Write a story in which you spill a secret, yours or someone else's. Disguise as necessary.
19. Write a story that takes place in an empty landscape.
20. Rewrite a scene from history.
21. Write a story that involves time travel.
22. Write a story that happens on a bicycle.
23. Write a story that contains elements of a real holiday memory.
24. Write a story that takes place over breakfast.
25. Write a story that includes a humiliation, real or invented.

26. Write a story that involves a celebrity.
27. Write a story in which the impossible is now possible.
28. Write a story with a theme of "The End."
29. Write a story that takes place in a hotel.
30. Write a story that incorporates a piece of scientific/analytic data.
31. Write a story that takes place late at night.
32. Write a story that is exactly 75 words long.
33. Write a story in the form of a review.
34. Write a story that includes a piece of real overheard dialogue.
35. Write a story where someone has an illness, real or invented.
36. Write a story that includes all four of these words: pineapple, beauty, bifocals, grass.
37. Write a story inspired by a story of your grandparent.
38. Write a story with a theme of escape.
39. Write a story that happens on the telephone.
40. Write a story around a compulsive behavior.
41. Write a story in the form of a fable.
42. Write a story in exactly 10 sentences.
43. Write a story where someone is lying.
44. Write a story that involves travel.
45. Write a story that takes place in extreme weather.
46. Write a story that involves a miracle.

47. Write a story that includes a strong smell.
48. Open the book nearest to you. Incorporate the first sentence you read into a story.
49. Write a story that goes to a dark/shadow place.
50. Write a story that takes place in the future.
51. Write a story that takes place in the past.
52. Write a story that references pop culture.
53. Write a story that includes a death or near death.
54. Write a story that takes place in November.
55. Write a story that begins at the end.
56. Write a story that includes some sort of election.
57. Write a story that takes place on a train.
58. Write a story that consists of only one sentence (any length).
59. Write a story that includes some sort of treasure.
60. Write a story that includes a scandal.
61. Write a story that features the color white.
62. Write a story that is inspired by an actual newspaper/magazine headline (I like to just read the headline and not the story).
63. Write a story told by an unreliable narrator.
64. Write a story that takes place during a storm.
65. Write a story in the form of a list.
66. Write a story that takes place in a fancy restaurant.
67. Write a story that includes some sort of unexplained phenomenon.

68. Write a story that includes the number 17.

69. Write a story on the theme of "my father" (doesn't have to be true).

70. Ask someone (anyone) to tell you a story. Use any part as inspiration for your own story.

71. Write a story where something is salvaged.

72. Write a story that includes a red sweater.

73. Write a story that involves a visitor.

74. Write a story that takes place in a church/ mosque/synagogue/temple.

75. Write a story that takes place on a holiday.

76. Write a story where something hidden is discovered.

77. Write a story where the narrator has a superpower.

78. Write a story where something is finished.

79. Write a story that takes place in a car.

80. Write a story where the weather changes, and this also changes the story.

81. Write a story in the form of a monologue (just one person speaking).

82. Write a story involving fire.

83. Write a story that includes (or at least mentions) a childhood toy.

84. Write a story in less than 100 words.

85. Write a story based on something that happened to you yesterday.

86. Write a story in the form of a Letter to the Editor.
87. Write a story involving an operation.
88. Write a story featuring the color orange.
89. Write a 13-word story.
90. Write a story that uses the device of repetition.
91. Write a story set in the summer.
92. Write a "Sweet 16" story.
93. Write a story that takes place while it's snowing.
94. Write a story using the 2nd person point of view (you).
95. Write a story that involves some sort of contest.
96. Write a story where someone is trying to hide something.
97. Write a story involving a wrongful accusation.
98. Write a story where something is found.
99. Write a story involving food.
100. Write a story with the theme "the day after."

# Author Acknowledgements

I'm deeply grateful to everyone who has allowed me to teach them.

To Sally Reno, Kona Morris, James Thomas, and Moria Woodruff, who read early drafts of this manuscript and helped me find my true center. To Patricia Morrison, who suggested I start teaching flash fiction workshops many years ago. To Kathy Fish, Rob Geisen, Jonathan Montgomery, Nick Morris, Leah Rogin-Roper, Randall Brown, Meg Tuite, Robert Vaughan, Len Kuntz, Karen Stefano, David Galef, Robert Scotellaro, Pam Painter, Kim Chinquee, Paul Beckman, Jayne Martin, Bryan Jansing, Selah Saterstrom, and everyone who has given me a stage and taught me how to be a better teacher and write a better book.

Thanks to everyone involved in Flash Fiction Retreats, the UK Flash Fiction Festival, The Fbomb Flash Fiction Reading Series, Bending Genres, Fast Forward Press, The Association of Writing and Writing Programs, the Community College of Denver, Arapahoe Community College and the University of Colorado Writing Center for giving me opportunities to create or refine various parts of this project. To all the organizations and colleagues that have inspired and hosted me—thank you.

My special thanks to Becky LeJeune and the Bond Literary Agency.

My deepest gratitude to Jude Higgins and Ad Hoc Fiction. And I'm totally excited and honored to have original artwork by Janice Leagra on the cover of this book. Thank you!

To all my teachers. Every one of you left a mark on the writer I was to become, especially my greatest teachers, Maiya Winter and Felix Kachadourian.

To my creative partner, Nick Busheff.

And finally, thank you, dear reader, for allowing me to share the form I love so much.

# About the Author

Nancy Stohlman has been a writer, editor, publisher, and professor for more than a decade. She's published multiple books of flash fiction and flash novels including *The Vixen Scream and Other Bible Stories* and *Madam Velvet's Cabaret of Oddities*, a finalist for a 2019 Colorado Book Award. Her work has been anthologized widely, appearing in the W.W. Norton *New Micro: Exceptionally Short Fiction*, Macmillan's *The Practice of Fiction*, and *The Best Small Fictions 2019*, as well as adapted for the stage. She teaches at the University of Colorado Boulder.

To inquire about booking Ms. Stohlman for a speaking engagement, please contact her directly.

nancystohlman.com
Facebook.com/nancy.stohlman
Twitter: @nancystohlman